How Did That Get Here?

# The Biography of Chocolate

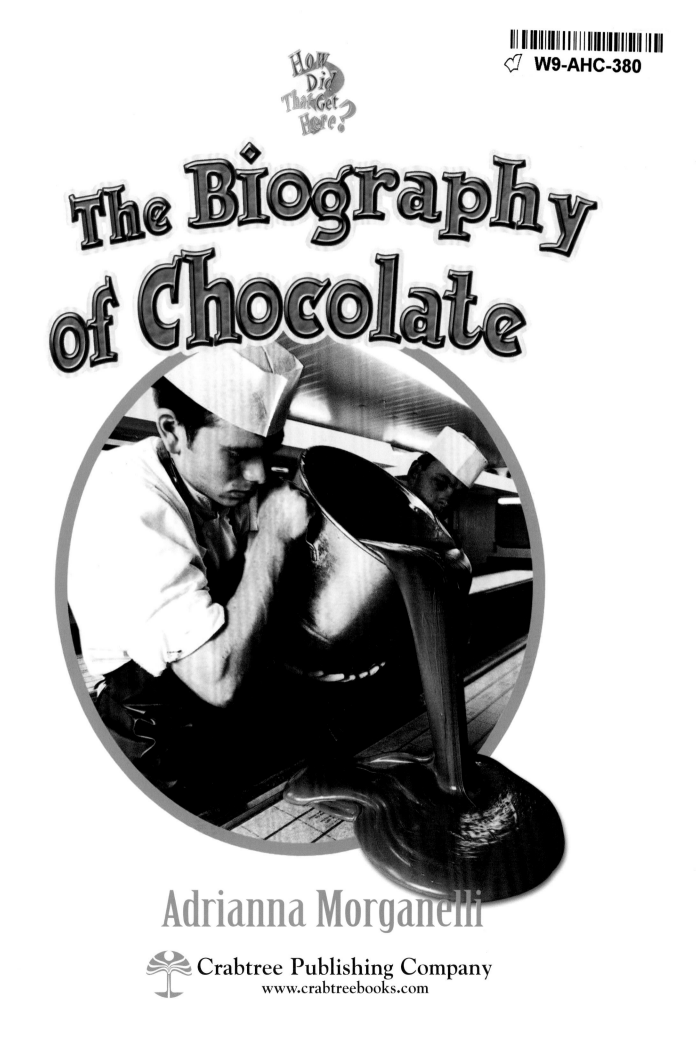

## Adrianna Morganelli

Crabtree Publishing Company
www.crabtreebooks.com

# Crabtree Publishing Company
### www.crabtreebooks.com

## For Charlene, the ultimate chocolate enthusiast

**Coordinating editor:** Ellen Rodger
**Project editor:** Carrie Gleason
**Editors:** Rachel Eagen, L. Michelle Nielsen
**Production coordinator:** Rosie Gowsell
**Layout and production assistance:** Samara Parent
**Art director:** Rob MacGregor
**Scanning technician:** Arlene Arch
**Photo research:** Allison Napier

**Consultant:** James D. McMahon Jr., Director and Senior Curator for the Hershey Museum

**Photo Credits:** AP Wide World Photos: p. 23, p. 28 (bottom), p. 31 (top); Werner Forman/Art Resource, NY: p. 10 (top right); Schalkwijk/Art Resource, NY: p. 11 (top); Bibliotheque Nationale, Paris, France, Lauros /Giraudon/Bridgeman Art Library: p. 16; Musee Nat. des Arts et Traditions Populaires, Paris, France, Archives Charmet/Bridgeman Art Library: p. 17 (top); Musee des Arts Decoratifs, Paris, France, Flammarion/Bridgeman Art Library: p. 13 (bottom); Museo de America, Madrid, Spain/Bridgeman Art Library: p. 4; Private Collection, Archives Charmet/ Bridgeman Art Library: p. 19 (top); Private Collection/Bridgeman Art Library: p. 21 (top); Private Collection, The Stapleton Collection/Bridgeman Art Library/All Rights Reserved: p. 12, p. 15 (top), p. 18; Bettmann/Corbis: p. 14, p. 21 (bottom); Keith

Dannemiller/Corbis: p. 7 (bottom left), p. 25 (top); Werner Forman/Corbis: p. 11 (bottom); Owen Franken/Corbis: p. 3, p. 24, p. 25 (bottom), p. 27 (both), p. 28 (top); Historical Picture Archive/Corbis: p. 13 (top); Hulton-Deutsch Collection/Corbis: p. 17 (bottom); Wolfgang Kaehler/Corbis: p. 8 (top); Krause, Johansen/A.B. /zefa/Corbis: p. 29 (middle right); Danny Lehman/Corbis: p. 5 (bottom); Les Pickett; Papilio/Corbis: p. 30; Richard T. Nowitz/Corbis: p. 26; Reuters/Corbis: p. 31 (bottom); C. Schmidt/zefa/Corbis: p. 29 (bottom right); Setboun/Corbis: p. 1; Dung Vo Trung/Corbis Sygma: cover; Underwood & Underwood/Corbis: p. 20; Mary Evans Picture Library: p. 15 (bottom); Karen Robinson/Panos Pictures: p. 22; Peter Bowater /Photo Researchers, Inc.: p. 9; Other images from stock cd

**Cartography:** Jim Chernishenko: p. 6

**Cover:** Chocolate is shaped and molded into many different forms, such as these sweet chocolate frogs.

**Title page:** A French chocolatier pours liquid chocolate onto a table where it will be shaped and hardened.

**Contents page:** Chocolate is made from cacao beans.

---

## Crabtree Publishing Company
www.crabtreebooks.com          1-800-387-7650

Printed in Canada/072019/MA20190417

**Library of Congress Cataloging-in-Publication Data**
Morganelli, Adrianna, 1979-
    The biography of chocolate / written by Adrianna Morganelli.
       p. cm. -- (How did that get here?)
ISBN-13: 978-0-7787-2481-0 (rlb)
ISBN-10: 0-7787-2481-6 (rlb)
ISBN-13: 978-0-7787-2517-6 (pbk)
ISBN-10: 0-7787-2517-0 (pbk)
    1. Cacao beans--Juvenile literature. 2. Cacao--Juvenile literature. 3. Chocolate--Juvenile literature. I. Title. II. Series.
SB267.M67 2005
633.7'4--dc22
                                                2005019020
                                                LC

**Published in Canada**
**Crabtree Publishing**
616 Welland Ave.
St. Catharines, Ontario
L2M 5V6

**Published in the United States**
**Crabtree Publishing**
PMB 59051
350 Fifth Avenue, 59th Floor
New York, New York 10118

**Published in the United Kingdom**
**Crabtree Publishing**
Maritime House
Basin Road North, Hove
BN41 1WR

**Published in Australia**
**Crabtree Publishing**
Unit 3 – 5
Currumbin Court
Capalaba QLD 4157

# Contents

# What is Chocolate?

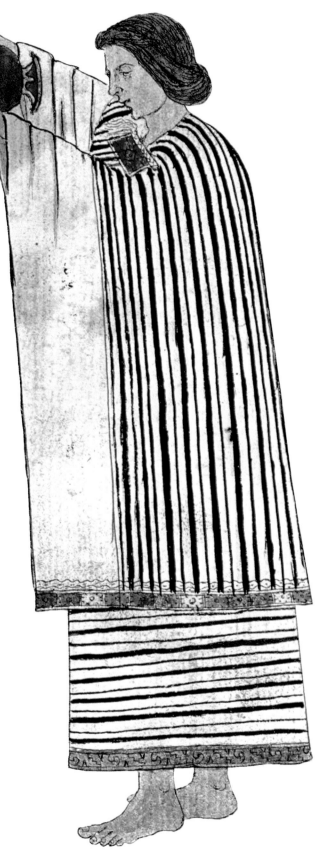

One of the world's sweetest treats, chocolate is a food made from the beans of the cacao tree. Cacao trees originated, or first grew, in the **rainforests** of South and Central America. It was first cultivated, or grown as a crop, by the ancient **Mesoamerican** peoples. They used cacao beans to create a frothy chocolate drink flavored with spices. Once Europeans discovered the cacao tree's secret, chocolate became an important **commodity**. Today, chocolate is a sweet indulgence enjoyed by people around the world. As the demand for chocolate continues to grow, scientists are racing to find ways to protect the world's supply of cacao from its shrinking rainforest home and from plant diseases that kill the crop.

## Chocolate Uses

Today, the two main chocolate products are cocoa for drinking and chocolate candy, but chocolate is also used as a flavoring for sauces and in many desserts, such as cookies, cakes, and brownies. Scientists have found that chocolate is a useful addition to some medicines as well. Cocoa butter, the fat from the cacao bean, is used in cosmetics, ointments, and as a coating for pills. After cacao beans are processed, the leftover **pods** are used in cattle feed and as garden mulch, and the **pulp** is added to some pet foods.

▶ *Many people regard the Maya of Central America as the world's first chocolatiers. A chocolatier is a person who is skilled at making chocolate.*

## Celebrate with Chocolate

Chocolate is often associated with many religious and national holidays and festive celebrations, where it is traditionally given as a gift to loved ones and friends. The demand for chocolate in North America is so great during holidays that manufacturing companies begin to produce chocolate far in advance. Halloween is the biggest holiday of the year for the chocolate industry, followed by Christmas and Easter. Chocolate is also a symbol of love and devotion. On Valentine's Day in North America, chocolate is given to a loved one.

▸ *The first solid chocolate was made in 1847 in England.*

## Dia de los Muertos

During the Mexican holiday *Dia de los Muertos*, or the Day of the Dead, cacao beans are ground with chilies, nuts, spices, and herbs to create a dish called *mole*. Families build *ofrendas*, or altars, in their homes and on gravesites to welcome the souls of departed loved ones. The *mole* is left on the altar with candles, photographs of the deceased, flowers, and a dish of cacao beans as an offering to the visiting spirits.

*Day of the Dead is a joyous holiday where people remember the deceased with parades, dancing, and chocolate!*

# Chocolate Lands

Scientists believe the cacao tree originated in the rainforests of South America, either in the upper Orinoco River region of Venezuela, or the Amazon basin of Brazil. As the demand for cocoa and chocolate grew, cacao trees were imported to new parts of the world to increase production. Today, cacao trees are grown in Mexico, Central and South America, Africa, Asia, and the Caribbean Islands. Cacao trees are cultivated on small farms, or on large farms called plantations that are owned by companies employing hundreds of workers.

## Growers and Consumers

About 15 million acres (six million hectares) of cacao trees are planted around the world. About 90 percent of cacao trees are grown by families with the help of some hired workers on less than 12 acres (five hectares) of land. Today, 70 percent of the world's cacao beans grow in West Africa, and almost half of the world's supply comes from the Ivory Coast. Europeans **consume** the most chocolate per person. Switzerland sells the most chocolate at about 24 pounds (11 kilograms) per person each year.

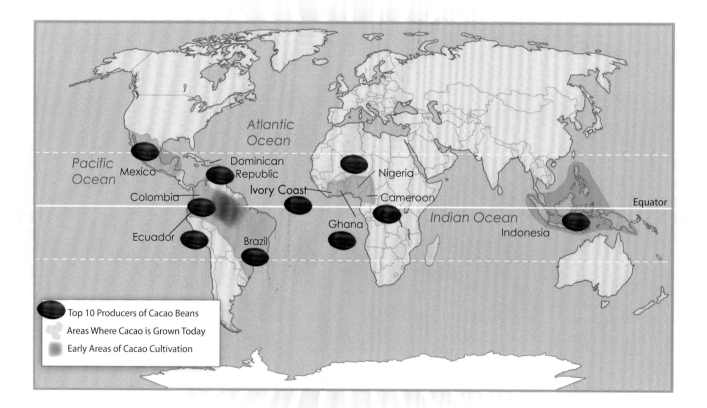

*Cacao beans can only be grown in the tropics. The area where the beans grow affects the amount of cocoa butter in the beans and also helps determine the taste. Chocolate companies use beans blended from different areas to achieve just the right flavor.*

## An Inside Look

Inside the cacao pod, the beans are protected by a fleshy white pulp. The pulp has to be scraped from the beans before chocolate can be made. Cacao beans naturally taste bitter and must undergo many processes to bring out the chocolate flavor.

(top and right) Cacao pods are the fruit of the cacao tree. Cacao pods grow up to 12 inches (30 cm) long and five inches (13 cm) in diameter, and have deep furrows on their surfaces.

## Types of Cacao Trees

There are different types of cacao trees. The main type is the forastero, which makes up 90 percent of the world's cacao crop. The forastero originated in the Amazon region of Brazil. Today, the tree is grown mostly in Brazil and West Africa. It produces dark purple cacao beans, or seeds, that are hardy and easy to grow for a high **yield**. The criollo cacao tree originated in Central America, and is grown in South America and Indonesia today. It yields less beans than the forastero tree, is more difficult to grow, and is more vulnerable to plant diseases. The criollo's yellowish-white bean has a mild flavor, and is used to produce high-quality chocolate.

# The Chocolate Tree

Cacao trees only grow in tropical rainforests close to the equator, where it is warm year-round. The trees need the high **humidity** and steady rainfall of the rainforest to survive. Wild cacao trees grow to a height of 30 to 40 feet (nine to 12 meters) and live for about 60 years. They thrive in the shade of larger trees, from which they receive moisture and protection from the sun and wind. Cacao trees absorb **nutrients** from decaying, or rotting, vegetation on the rainforest floor. Tiny insects, called midges, **pollinate** the trees' flowers to produce pods. New cacao trees begin to grow once the cacao beans **germinate** on the rainforest floor. Cacao beans do not fall naturally to the ground when they are ripe.

*The pink and white flowers of the cacao tree grow in small clusters on the branches and trunk.*

◄ *When rainforest animals, such as bats, macaws, and monkeys, gnaw through the pods to eat the pulp, the cacao beans fall to the ground. The beans take root in the soil and grow into new trees.*

## Cacao Pods

The flowers and fruit, or pods, of the cacao tree grow directly from the tree's branches and trunk and not the branch tips as they do on most trees. A cacao tree yields about 50 pods twice a year. The pods take five to six months to ripen, and change color from green to red, orange, or yellow. Inside each pod are about 20 to 40 beans covered in a white waxy flesh called pulp. Chocolate is made from beans after they have been removed from the pulp.

## Growing on Plantations

On cacao plantations, cacao beans are grown in a nursery until they are four to six months old. The **seedlings** are then planted seven to ten feet (two to three meters) apart in baskets or plastic bags. In about a month, the seedlings are large enough to be **transplanted** to fields beneath the shade of larger trees, such as banana, rubber, pimiento, coconut, and cassava trees. After three years, cacao trees begin to grow pods. Over the next five years, the trees produce increasing numbers of pods. Plantation workers keep cacao trees pruned, or trimmed, to a height of about 25 feet (eight meters) to make it easier to gather the ripe pods at the tops of the trees. Farmers and workers check the crops regularly for diseases, pests, and molds that could destroy an entire harvest.

## Sun Plantations

Sun plantations grow only cacao trees. When the trees are old enough to flower, the surrounding shade trees are cut down. This leaves the cacao tree exposed to the sun's full strength. Cacao trees that are grown in the sun produce a higher yield than cacao trees grown beneath shade trees. Cacao trees on sun plantations are prone to pests and diseases because they are taken out of their natural rainforest habitat, where plants, mammals, and insects eat harmful pests. Cacao trees that grow naturally in the rainforest without the use of chemicals to keep pests away are used to make **organic** chocolate.

*On sun plantations, smaller numbers of trees are pollinated by midges because they are less common in sunny fields. Instead, workers grow new trees in nurseries.*

9

# The First Chocolate Cultivators

**Archaeologists** believe the Native peoples of Mexico and Central America, or Mesoamericans, were the first to enjoy chocolate. The cacao tree grew wild in the rainforests where the ancient Maya lived, in what is now southern Mexico. The Maya were the first to plant cacao on plantations. Many Maya artifacts, such as sculptures, wall murals, and ceramic vases, show people collecting cacao, and kings, gods, and animals drinking chocolate. All Maya drank chocolate, but wealthy Maya drank the beverage from elaborate vessels. Chocolate was also used in religious ceremonies.

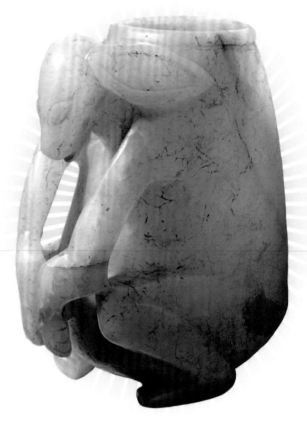

▲ *Wealthy Mesoamericans drank chocolate from elaborate cups, such as this hare-shaped drinking vessel.*

*Some archaeologists believe that Olmec people were the first to use cacao. The Olmec lived in southern Mexico and Central America about 3,000 years ago, and built large stone heads. The Olmec broke open ripe cacao pods to make a drink from the sweet pulp inside.*

## How the Maya Made Chocolate

To make chocolate, the Maya **fermented** and dried the cacao beans, then roasted them over a fire. After removing the shells, the beans were ground into a chocolate paste by crushing them with a small stone called a mano against a stone surface called a metate. They added water, chili peppers, herbs, honey, and vanilla to the paste and poured the mixture back and forth from cup to pot until a thick froth formed on top. This process mixed the fatty part of the bean into the drink so that it would not settle on top.

## The Aztecs

By the 1400s, the Aztec people controlled a territory of Mesoamerica that stretched from northern Mexico to the Maya lands. The Aztecs could not grow cacao trees in the dry highlands of what is now central Mexico, so they traded with the Maya for cacao beans. The Aztecs made frothy chocolate beverages as the Maya did. They also added cornmeal and wine to the drink, called chocolatl, and served it cold flavored with vanilla beans, pimiento, and chili peppers. Only wealthy Aztecs, such as nobles, rulers, priests, warriors, and merchants could afford to buy the beans. Aztecs also used cacao beans as currency. People in the Aztec **empire** paid a tribute, or tax, of cacao beans to their rulers.

*(right) A mural in present-day Mexico City shows ancient Mesoamericans gathering and trading cacao beans.*

## Gift of the Gods

According to ancient Aztec legend, a white-skinned, bearded god named Quetzalcoatl, the god of wisdom and knowledge, came from his land of gold to present the people with the seeds of the cacao tree. He taught them how to grow the cacao tree, to harvest its pods, and to prepare chocolatl.

*A shell mosaic of the Aztec god Quetzalcoatl.*

11

# A Sweet European Discovery

Beginning in the 1500s, Spanish **conquistadors** sailed to Central and South America to take control of the land and its riches. Among the riches they discovered were cacao beans. When conquistador Hernán Cortés arrived in the Aztec city of Tenochtitlán in 1519, the emperor, Montezuma II, and his people welcomed Cortés with great feasts and served him chocolatl. Cortés wrote about the drink in a letter to Spain's king. He described chocolate's power to give energy, and the gold cups in which it was served. In 1528, Cortés returned to Spain and presented the king with cacao beans and the Mayan method of making the beans into a chocolate drink.

## Spain's Valuable Secret

Chocolate soon became a popular drink in Spain and with the Spanish colonists, or settlers, in Mexico. For nearly 100 years, Spain kept chocolate's source a secret because of the money Spain made as the only supplier of chocolate to Europe. The Spanish first prepared the beverage cold, and frothed it as the Mesoamericans had with a carved wooden tool called a *molinillo*. The beverage was later served hot in chocolate pots that had holes in the lids for the *molinillos*. To combat chocolate's bitter flavor, the Spanish added sugar to the drink. Cacao beans and sugar were very expensive imports, so only the wealthy could afford to buy them. Vanilla, aniseed, nutmeg, cloves, orange and rose water, and cinnamon were also added for flavor.

◄ *Montezuma was the last Aztec emperor. After Cortés arrived, a period of conquest took place. The Spanish took over Aztec land and ruled over the people.*

*Many European chocolate houses admitted only men, but others allowed anyone in who could afford to pay for the sweet chocolate drink as well as the entrance fee.*

## Spreading Throughout Europe

The popularity of drinking chocolate spread quickly through Europe. In 1606, an Italian merchant visited Spain and brought the custom of drinking chocolate back to Italy. From Italy, chocolate spread to Austria and Holland. When Spanish princess Anne of Austria married France's King Louis XIII in 1615, she brought cacao beans to Paris and introduced them to the French **court**. Spanish **monks** offered the beverage to visitors from other countries.

## London's Chocolate Houses

In 1657, the first chocolate shop opened in London, England. Chocolate houses, where wealthy men paid an entrance fee to drink hot chocolate, gamble, play cards, eat, socialize, and discuss politics, became fashionable in London. Some chocolate houses also sold tickets for operas. As chocolate became more available, it became more affordable, and **working-class** men began to visit chocolate houses as well to enjoy the sweet drink.

◀ *During the 1600s and 1700s, fancy chocolate pots made of silver, gold, and porcelain were used to serve hot chocolate drinks. Most chocolate pots had a hole in the lid to accommodate the* **molinillos.**

# Chocolate Spreads

Spain was the first country to control the cacao trade between Europe and the Americas. The Spanish built cacao plantations on islands throughout the Caribbean, in the Philippines, and in Central and South America where they set up colonies and sent the cacao trees to be transplanted. By 1810, Spain's cacao plantations in Venezuela produced half of the world's cacao.

## Growing European Plantations

When other European countries learned where chocolate came from, new cacao-growing colonies were established and Spain began to lose control of the chocolate trade. Europeans wanted to control their own cacao plantations so they did not have to buy cacao beans from Spain. In 1560, Dutch sailors brought cacao trees from Venezuela to their colonies in Celebes, present-day Sulawesi in Indonesia. By the 1620s, the Dutch had also established cacao plantations in other areas of Indonesia, Venezuela, and their colonies in the Caribbean. England established colonies in Ceylon, which is present-day Sri Lanka, and began shipping cacao beans to other European countries from its plantations. France began cultivating cacao trees in Martinique and St. Lucia in the Caribbean, and Madagascar off the coast of Africa.

◀ *Europeans brought plants discovered in other lands to plantations in their colonies. Plants they brought included cacao trees from Central America, tea from China, and coffee from Ethiopia.*

## Chocolate Moves to Africa

The Portuguese established colonies in Brazil, and shipped cacao beans to the islands of Príncipe and São Tomé, both off the West Coast of Africa. By the 1890s, many cacao plantations thrived on the islands, and they became the world's leading cacao producers. Cacao trees spread from São Tomé to Spain's colonies on the nearby island of Fernando Po. In 1879, an African plantation worker smuggled seedlings from Fernando Po across the Gulf of Guinea and planted them on a British plantation on the Gold Coast, in present-day Ghana. From there, cacao trees spread to France's colonies along the Ivory Coast and into Nigeria. Today, the Ivory Coast is the world's leading supplier of chocolate.

▲ *As greater amounts of cacao beans became available in Europe, the cost of chocolate was gradually lowered so that more people could enjoy it.*

*(above) On cacao plantations in their colonies, Europeans used local people to do the work.*

# Cacao Slavery

From the mid-1500s to the late 1800s, the Spanish forced Mesoamericans into slavery, harvesting and processing cacao beans on Spanish plantations. Slaves were prevented from living in their villages, and were not paid for their labor. Many were beaten and forced to work long hours. Mesoamerican slaves were first used to harvest cacao in Mexico and Guatemala, and later in Venezuela and Ecuador. Spanish plantation owners used slaves so that they could make more money by not paying workers.

## African Slaves

Many Mesoamericans died from diseases brought by Europeans. This created a labor shortage on plantations. The shortage was met by bringing in slaves from Africa. Thousands of African slaves worked on cacao plantations in the Caribbean, and Central and South America. The Dutch imported about 100,000 African slaves a year to their colonies in the Caribbean, and traded them to plantation owners to work on cacao and other food crop plantations.

*The demand for chocolate was great in Spain, so Spanish soldiers took control of the Aztec's cacao supply and forced them to work on plantations.*

CHOCOLAT GUÉRIN-BOUTRON

BOTANIQUE ILLUSTRÉE
84 sujets variés

Le Cacaoyer. — Chocolat. Cacao. Bonbons.

*(above) A trading card from a French chocolate company shows a slave harvesting cacao while a European oversees his work on a plantation in Africa.*

## Taking a Stand on Slavery

Portugal's plantations on the islands of São Tomé and Príncipe, off the African coast, were worked by slaves from Angola, Africa. Most European countries ended slavery in their colonies by the late 1800s. By 1901, rumors of the harsh working conditions on the Portuguese plantations reached the European chocolate companies that bought the islands' crops. The Cadbury chocolate company, supported by chocolate companies in England and Germany, tried to persuade the Portuguese government and plantation owners to end slavery. When the working conditions on the islands did not improve, Cadbury and other chocolate companies in America and Europe announced that they would no longer purchase cacao from Portuguese plantations.

*(right) An African worker in Cameroon harvests cacao using a long pole.*

# Birth of the Chocolate Industry

Until the mid-1700s, chocolate was a handmade product that was time consuming and expensive to produce. During a period of history called the **Industrial Revolution**, machines were invented that changed the way people worked. These machines made it possible to quickly and easily produce solid chocolate for eating. This made chocolate more affordable for everyone. The chocolate mill was an important invention that quickly ground large amounts of cacao beans.

## Van Houten's Cocoa

Before the Industrial Revolution, chocolate drinks had a gritty texture and a greasy appearance. The cocoa butter, or fat of the cacao beans, left an oily substance on the surface. In 1828, Dutch chemist Coenraad van Houten invented a press to remove about two-thirds of the cocoa butter from chocolate liquor, or the paste ground from cacao beans. Once the cocoa butter was removed, a hard cake of chocolate was left behind. Van Houten ground the cake into a fine powder and called it cocoa. Europeans embraced cocoa, finding it easier to use to make cakes and candies. Van Houten sold cocoa to candy makers, housewives, and bakers.

*(right) As chocolate became easier and less expensive to produce and buy, companies created advertisements that targeted women and children. Advertisements encouraged people to buy breakfast chocolate, and claimed that eating chocolate bars boosted energy.*

prenez du Cacao
**Van Houten**

## The Chocolate Bar is Born!

In 1847, John and Benjamin Cadbury and Joseph Fry discovered a way to use cocoa butter to make solid chocolate. They found that by adding an amount of cocoa butter to chocolate liquor and sugar, chocolate could be molded into a form that remained solid at room temperature. Their discovery resulted in the first chocolate, or candy, bar.

## Improving Taste and Texture

Chocolate makers also worked to improve the taste and texture of chocolate. In 1875, Swiss inventor Daniel Peter created smooth and creamy milk chocolate. He combined cocoa with condensed milk, which was created by Swiss inventor Henri Nestlé. Condensed milk is a sweet, thick milk. In 1893 in Switzerland, Rodolphe Lindt invented conching, a way of making chocolate smoother. Conching **kneaded** the chocolate, blending in all the cocoa grains, so that chocolate was no longer gritty.

▸ *Workers making chocolate in a European factory in the 1900s.*

## Chocolate Chip Cookies

In 1930, Ruth Wakefield accidentally invented chocolate chip cookies while baking at her inn, The Toll House, in Massachusetts, in the United States. When Wakefield ran out of cocoa powder, she broke a bar of Nestlé's chocolate in pieces with the belief that the chocolate would blend with the dough to make chocolate cookies. She discovered that the chocolate pieces did not completely melt. Her cookie became known as the Toll House Cookie. When Nestlé began to sell chocolate chips, the Toll House Cookie recipe was printed on the package.

# Big Chocolate Companies

With the invention of solid chocolate, many chocolate factories were built in Europe and North America. The first chocolate factory in the United States opened when Irish chocolate maker John Hannon imported cacao beans into Dorchester, Massachusetts, from the Caribbean. In 1765, Hannon, working with Dr. James Baker, opened a chocolate mill to process the cacao beans into chocolate. At the mill, cacao beans were ground into chocolate liquor, and pressed into cakes to be made into drinking chocolate. Their company was named Hannon's Best Chocolate. After Hannon was lost at sea during a voyage to the Caribbean to buy more cacao, the company was renamed the Baker Company.

## Cadbury

In 1824, a **Quaker** named John Cadbury established a chocolate factory in Birmingham, England. Chocolate was favored by Quakers because they did not approve of alcoholic drinks. By 1854, Cadbury was the sole chocolate supplier to England's Queen Victoria. Cadbury's sons took over the business in 1866. They purchased Conraad van Houten's press for the factory and began to sell their own cocoa powder. The Cadburys built a town for their employees called the Bournville Village. The company provided homes and medical facilities for employees.

*(below) During World War I, the United States army hired American chocolate manufacturers to ship blocks of chocolate to soldiers in Europe. The soldiers developed a taste for chocolate candy and when they returned home at the end of the war, the demand for chocolate candy bars grew.*

(above) An advertisement for Cadbury's boxed chocolates from the early 1900s. Chocolate companies today compete with each other to sell the most chocolate.

(below) **Hershey's Kisses** chocolates coming off the line at the Hershey factory in the 1930s.

## Hershey

In 1886, after several business failures, Milton Hershey achieved his first business success making caramels. After seeing a display of chocolate-making equipment at the 1893 Columbian Exposition in Chicago, Hershey decided to dedicate part of his caramel company to the manufacturing of chocolate and cocoa. In 1900 he sold his first milk chocolate bars. Five years later, he opened what became the largest chocolate factory in the world in the town of Hershey, Pennsylvania. Hershey believed that fairness and good working conditions for employees were important so he built his planned community complete with worker-owned homes and a trolley system to bring workers from nearby towns.

# West African Chocolate

Large chocolate factories throughout the world use about a million tons (907,185 tonnes) of cacao beans a year from West Africa's Ivory Coast. Cacao farmers and plantation workers work long hours cutting cacao pods from the trees with long, sharp knives, and carry heavy loads. Farmers rely on **brokers** and **multinational companies** to sell their harvests. After selling the cacao beans on the world market, brokers keep most of the profits, and the farmers receive very little money. Most cacao farmers cannot afford machinery, or to hire many workers to help harvest their crops. In some cases, workers receive little pay for their labor, and others receive only food and lodging. Most of the money that consumers pay for their chocolate is used for manufacturing, packaging, shipping, advertising, and profits for retailers.

▸ *A small amount of the money that consumers pay for chocolate reaches cacao growers and workers. Some people argue that if consumers paid more for their chocolate, then farmers might receive more money.*

## Child Labor

In the 1980s, **child labor activists** reported that children were working on some West African plantations, growing and harvesting cacao. The child workers gathered pods from the trees, carried heavy loads of cacao beans, and cleared fields for new plantations. In many cases, the families of the child workers were very poor. The children could not attend school because the money they earned was needed to help support their families.

## The Help of Chocolate Manufacturers — Fair Trade

Some chocolate manufacturers around the world are working to end poor labor practices by refusing to buy cacao from plantations where workers are not paid well. Instead, these chocolate manufacturers pay for fair trade cacao. Fair trade is a movement that was established in 1988 that ensures that workers receive high enough wages for their labor to pay for food, shelter, health care, and education. Fair trade cacao also helps small farmers who receive a better price for the sale of their crop. The fair trade movement works for the care of the environment, and encourages consumers to be aware of the conditions under which a product is made.

*Many farmers and cacao plantation workers on Africa's Ivory Coast have never tasted chocolate because they cannot afford to buy the finished product.*

Large crops of cacao are usually harvested twice a year. Ripe pods are carefully removed from the cacao tree by hand with long poles that have hooks on the end. Workers are careful to avoid injuring the flowers and the young pods that are still ripening on the tree. After collecting the pods in baskets, workers split them open with a machete, or long knife, or with a quick blow from a stick. The beans and the pulp are scooped out of the cacao pods by hand.

*(above) A woman harvests a cacao pod with a machete on a cacao plantation.*

## Fermentation

Raw cacao beans are tough and bitter and need to ferment to bring out the natural scent and taste of chocolate. The beans and pulp are placed inside wooden boxes, sacks, or barrels and covered with leaves, such as banana leaves. They are then left in the hot sun for four to seven days. The heat causes the beans to lose their moisture, and they change color from purple or white to deep brown. The pulp begins to liquefy, or turn from a solid to a liquid, and is loosened from the beans. The longer the beans are left to ferment, the better the flavor and the greater the cost of the chocolate.

*(above) After the pods are cut from the tree, they are shelled to remove the beans from the pulp.*

*(below) As the beans dry, they become darker brown. Their flavor develops over time.*

## Drying

Once the beans have fermented, they are spread out to dry on the ground or on long tables in the sun for about a week. They are raked and turned over every few days so that they dry evenly. The beans are moved beneath overhangs to shelter them from the rain. In very wet climates, the beans are dried in artificial dryers that blow hot air at them through large drums.

## Selling Cacao

Dried beans are packed into bags weighing about 140 pounds (64 kilograms) each and sold to brokers. The price that the farmers receive is determined after the beans have been inspected for their quality. The price of cacao rises when there is a high demand for chocolate, or when plant diseases or drought limit the amount available for sale. When farmers harvest more cacao than consumers can buy, the price they receive for their cacao beans falls.

# From Bean to Bar

There are several stages of processing that cacao beans undergo to be made into chocolate. Roasting is the most important step in processing. During roasting, the chocolate flavor and aroma fully develop. The beans are cleaned of stones, leaves, and sand, by passing through electric vacuums, brushes, and sieves. The beans are then separated according to size and quality. Larger beans must be roasted longer. Beans are roasted in revolving drums at temperatures between 225°F and 300°F (107°C and 148°C) for 15 to 20 minutes. The cacao beans lose their water content, and the beans and their shells become dry and brittle.

## Winnowing

After roasting, the cacao beans are placed on a winnowing machine, where the shells, or husks, of the beans are cracked open to reveal the nibs, or centers of the beans. The nibs are then ground by machines that crush them between heavy stone or metal disks. The grinding, or milling, causes the fat of the nibs, called the cocoa butter, to melt. The result is a rich, dark paste called chocolate liquor, which hardens when it cools.

*(above) Cacao beans arrive at the chocolate factory in large bags.*

## Conching

The chocolate liquor is mixed with ingredients such as milk, sugar, and vanilla and is ground again in conches, or troughs, to get rid of the mixture's gritty texture. The conch machine gets its name from the conch shell-like appearance of its ribbed bed and rollers. Steel or **granite** rollers rotate over the mixture to smooth out the particles, or tiny bits, of chocolate and sugar.

*(right) Cocoa butter is also sold to manufacturers of skin oils and lotions, soaps, and creams for use in their products.*

*(below) Chocolate liquor is the ground up nibs of cacao beans.*

## Tempering

After conching, chocolate manufacturers put chocolate through another process called tempering. The chocolate mixture is heated to about 150°F (65°C), and then gradually cooled. This is done to give the chocolate a glossy sheen, and to prevent the cocoa butter from **crystallizing** and ruining the chocolate's smooth texture. Some tempered chocolate is shipped in liquid form, but most is molded into bars to be packaged and shipped to distributors and manufacturers who use solid chocolate in creating their products.

*(right) When hardened, some chocolate liquor is shipped to chocolatiers from the chocolate factory.*

*To make these chocolate rabbits, machines squirt liquid chocolate into molds along an assembly line.*

# Types of Chocolate

## 1. Sweet or Dark Chocolate

Sweet or dark chocolate contains chocolate liquor, a high content of cocoa butter and sugar, and little or no milk.

## 2. Semisweet Chocolate

Semisweet chocolate is made of chocolate liquor, cocoa butter, and sugar. This chocolate is used to make chocolate-covered candy, and in baking cookies and cakes.

## 3. Unsweetened Chocolate

Unsweetened chocolate, commonly known as baking chocolate, is cooled and hardened chocolate liquor. This chocolate has a low content of sugar, and its bitter taste makes it unsuitable for eating by itself. It is used as an ingredient in baking desserts.

## 4. Milk Chocolate

Milk chocolate is made of chocolate liquor, cocoa butter, sugar, condensed milk, and other flavorings. It is used to make many desserts and candy bars.

## 5. White Chocolate

White chocolate is made of cocoa butter, milk, sugar, and other flavorings. White chocolate is not technically chocolate because it does not contain any chocolate liquor. This chocolate has a mild flavor and is used to make desserts.

# A Bitter End to Chocolate

The world's supply of chocolate is in danger because the rainforests where cacao trees grow are being destroyed. Rainforests are cleared to provide land for grazing cattle, farms, logging, mining operations, and road building. Many rainforest trees are burned for fuel, and tropical **timber**, such as mahogany, teak, and rosewood, are used to make furniture and in building materials. The destruction of the rainforest results in the **extinction** of many plants and animals that thrive there, such as cacao.

*Large areas of rainforest have been cut down on Africa's Ivory Coast.*

## Frosty Pod

Plant diseases hurt cacao production. The chocolate industry estimates diseases destroy between 35 to 40 percent of cacao crops each year. *Moniliophthora rorei*, a fungus commonly known as frosty pod rot, infects cacao beans and leaves the pods swollen and covered in shiny white **spores**. Frosty pod rot kills cacao trees in South America, but scientists fear that countries in Central America and the Caribbean are at risk as well. There is no way to stop the disease yet, but removing infected cacao pods can help control the spread of the disease.

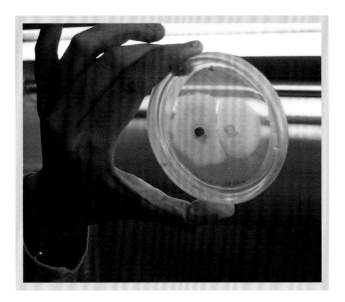

*(above) A scientist in a laboratory holds a sample of a fungus that kills cacao trees.*

## Witch's Broom

Witch's broom is a disease caused by a fungus called Crinipellis perniciosa. It deforms the branches of the cacao tree and shrivels cacao pods. Witch's Broom makes the pods brown and dry, and destroys the beans inside. The disease has attacked cacao trees in Central and South America. In Brazil, the production of cacao beans has dropped from 400,000 to 100,000 tons (362,874 to 90,718 tonnes) in the past ten years because of witch's broom. Despite scientists' research efforts, witch's broom is almost impossible to control. Pesticides and strains of cacao that can withstand witch's broom have been developed, but scientists fear that frosty pod rot could still infect the trees.

*(right) A cacao farmer in Venezuela checks his cacao pods for disease.*

## Black Pod

Black pod disease is caused by a fungus and infects all parts of the cacao tree. The disease is a serious problem in all areas of the world where cacao trees are grown. Black pod causes a brown sore to spread over the entire cacao pod, which causes it to turn black. It can take several days for the beans inside to become infected, and sometimes they are harvested in time. Diseased cacao beans are discolored and dried up. Recently, black pod has been severe in Central and West Africa. Efforts to control the disease include frequent harvesting, regular pruning, and use of **fungicides**.

# Glossary

**archaeologist** A person who studies ancient cultures

**broker** An agent who buys and sells for others

**child labor activist** A person or organization who reports on child workers and tries to end child labor

**commodity** A good that is bought and sold

**conquest** Forced takeover of a land or people

**conquistador** A Spanish explorer from the 1500s

**consume** To eat, drink or use up something

**court** The group of friends, family, and advisors to a king or queen

**crystallize** To form into small crystal-like shapes

**empire** A group of countries or states under one ruler

**extinct** No longer in existence

**ferment** The breaking down of a substance

**fungicides** Chemicals sprayed on plants to kill fungi

**germinate** To sprout or grow roots

**granite** A type of hard rock used for building

**humidity** The amount of moisture in the air

**Industrial Revolution** A period of social change starting in the late 1700s in England in which people began to move into cities to work in factories

**knead** To mix a substance by folding and stretching

**Mesoamerican** The people of Mexico and Central America

**monks** Religious men who usually live apart from the rest of society

**multinational company** A company that does business in more than one country

**nutrient** Substances that help living things grow

**organic** Crops that are grown without chemical fertilizers or pesticides

**pollinate** To transfer pollen from one plant to another to produce new seeds

**pod** The part of a plant that contains seeds

**pulp** The soft fleshy part of a fruit or vegetable

**Quaker** A member of a religious community called the Religious Society of Friends that was started in England in the 1600s

**rainforest** A tropical forest that receives a lot of rainfall

**seedling** A young plant

**spore** A cell produced by fungus that can grow and become a fully developed fungi

**timber** Wood for building

**transplant** To move a plant from one area to another

**working class** Laborers in society who depend on their wages for survival

**yield** The amount produced

# Index